Gracie's Story

Julie Schommer

Parson's Porch Books

Gracie's Story

ISBN: Softcover 978-1-949888-15-7

Copyright © 2014 by Julie Schommer

All rights reserved. No part of this book may be reproduced or transmitted in any form or by any means, electronic or mechanical, including photocopying, recording, or by any information storage and retrieval system, without permission in writing from the publisher.

To order additional copies of this book, contact:

Parson's Porch Books
1-423-475-7308
www.parsonsporch.com

Parson's Porch Books is an imprint of Parson's Porch & Company (PP&C) in Cleveland, Tennessee. PP&C is an innovative non-profit organization which raises money by publishing books of noted authors, representing all genres. All donations from contributors and profits from publishing are shared with the poor

Thank you to my moma for encouraging me to write this…

The Lord bless you and keep you.

The Lord make His face to shine upon you, and be gracious to you. Numbers 6:24-25

Gracie Schommer

Gracie's Story

I want to share an amazing story, a story about God's amazing Grace. God has given me a new life. He did so because he died on the cross for me and for you. I accepted Jesus Christ as my personal Lord and Savior at the age of 19 years old. I was at home and it was late at night. God hears our prayers at any time and any day! We can call on him any time! So my Christian life began.

The real story here begins many years later, when after several wonderful and healthy children, I became pregnant with a baby girl. I knew right away I wanted her name to be Gracie. Now during this pregnancy, I felt strongly that God was giving this child to us for a reason, though I knew not why. But I later realized why. It was to prove God had a plan and to prove he's still in the miracle business.

Pregnancy

While pregnant with Gracie, the doctor realized I had a blood clotting disorder and ordered daily shots of a blood thinner. Without these daily shots, I could have formed a blood clot and passed it on to my unborn baby, which would have caused her to die. Other than this, our baby girl seemed perfectly healthy.

I kept all my appointments to assure our baby girl was born healthy and well. All tests, including ultra sounds, looked good. At 37 weeks gestation, an amniocentesis was done to check for lung maturity. The test results said they were not mature. This test was repeated one week later. It still resulted in not mature. So at 39 weeks gestation, baby Gracie was born via C-section. She was beautiful with big, chunky cheeks. One of the nurses in the operating room even made the comment that "four pounds of her was in her cheeks." She weighed in at 8 pounds 1.7 ounces and was 20 ¾ inches long. What a beauty she was and oh how I thanked God for getting her safely delivered.

Perfect Little Girl

Gracie was perfect in every way-or so we thought. Gracie was a poor eater and did a lot of spitting up. Often babies do this, but they are perfectly fine. So no red light went off. She began to get a little yellow, a condition called jaundice. On day two, although she was still somewhat yellow, they decided to discharge us, but only with the agreement that she would see the pediatrician the next day. So we take our newest bundle of joy home.

You see, we already had two older girls, Lauren and Brittany and two boys, Cody and Robert. Gracie made number six, because her baby brother, Justin, died for unknown reasons two weeks before he was due to be delivered. Though I often think, had Justin lived, we would not have had Gracie. I had planned to have my tubes tied after his birth. But since he didn't make it, we left the option open, and therefore had Gracie. I know all things happen for a reason, but sometimes it's just hard to understand why. So I try not to question why.

We made it home and settled baby Gracie in. The next day, as promised, we took Gracie to the pediatrician's office. He visually looked at her and said she looked oaky, but did no blood test which is the only way to get a bilirubin level. He sent her home, but the next day a nurse from the pediatrician's office called saying Gracie's level needed to be tested that same day. I was confused since the doctor said she was okay. The nurse said, "You must take her in."

I later found out that same nurse questioned this doctor's judgment. Gracie was so yellow, and the nurse took it upon herself to insure she was tested. We are so very grateful for the nurse, because it turned out Gracie's level was high.

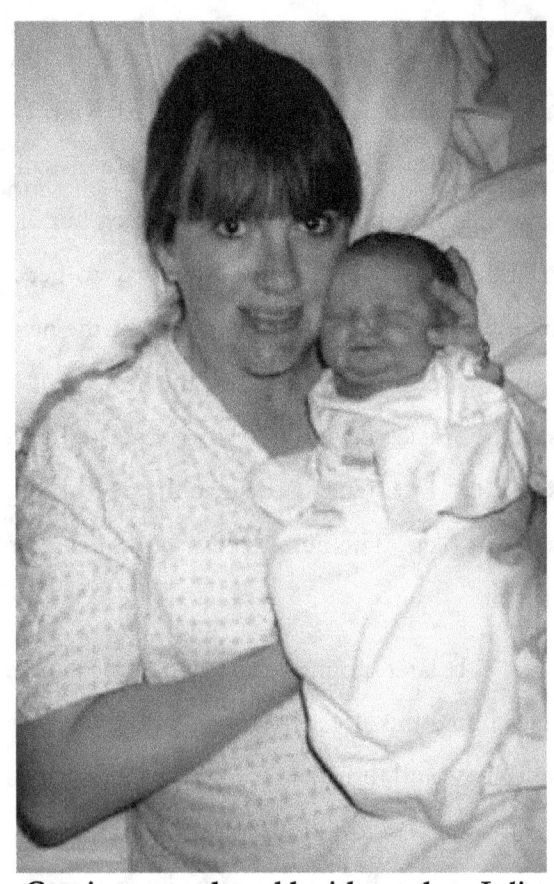

Gracie at one day old with mother, Julie

Home Health Care

So home health care was called to immediately deliver a bilirubin bed to our home. It resembled a tiny tanning bed with lots of bright bulbs. Gracie had to lie in this bed all of the time with nothing on but a diaper and eye protection. The only time we were allowed to take her out was to feed and change her. So we had little contact with her.

Since Gracie was a poor eater, we had begun keeping a log of how much she drank. My husband slept on the couch to keep an eye on Gracie while she lay in her "tanning bed."

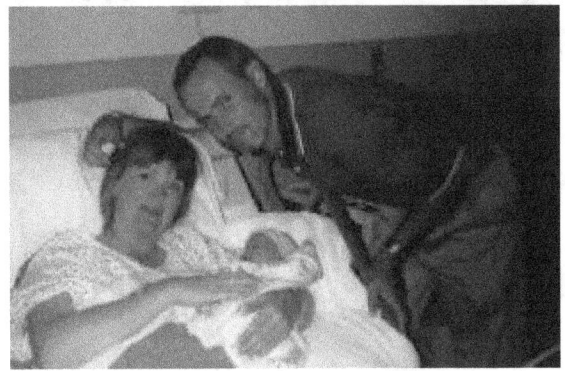

Gracie with Mom and Dad

On the second night, I never heard Gracie cry. When I got up on this Sunday morning, I asked if she slept well. He said she did and that she ate very well. In fact, she ate the best she ever had, so we were excited about that, little did we know at that time but later found out we were actually hurting her every time she drank her formula.

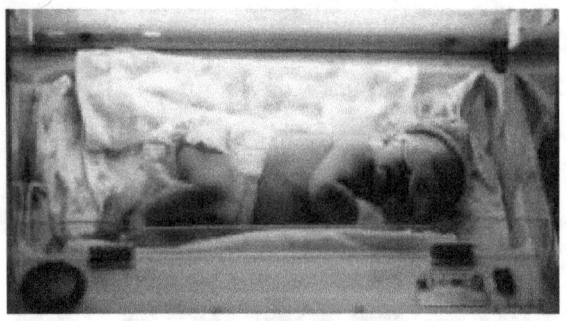

**Gracie at 5 days old in the
Bilirubin bed at home**

Something's Not Right

I sat on the couch on a Sunday morning just watching her sleep in this bright bed and thought something didn't seem right to me, the way she was breathing. Her breathing was rapid, and she made sounds each time she inhaled. I got the bulb syringe out thinking maybe her nose needed to be blown, but nothing came out, so I continued to sit on the couch, all the while wondering, is something wrong or am I just worrying for nothing.

I felt I should call the pediatrician, but since this was a Sunday I had to call in and wait for the doctor to get the page then return my call.

I didn't have to wait long until the doctor called. I explained how she was doing, he had me count her respirations (how many times she would breath) the number was high so he asked if I was counting inhales and exhales I said only inhales, he was concerned because it was so high. I tried to explain the sounds she was making. As she breathed, it was loud, so I asked if he wanted me to place the phone near her so he could listen. He did, so I placed the phone to her mouth. He was concerned and wanted us to take her to the hospital for evaluation.

Another Hospital Stay

We began to pack things up to take her to the hospital. Just before leaving, we noticed Gracie was no longer blinking. We even took our finger very close to her eye, and she still did not blink. We could not get her to take any of her bottle. Worry began to set in.

I know God says we should not worry we should put it in his hands, but I fail at this sometimes and know this is something I must work on. By the time we arrived at the emergency room at children's hospital in Knoxville, Gracie had become totally unresponsive. When the doctor pinched her toes and she did not respond, he told us a lot was going to happen very quickly, and it did. The nurses came in, scooped her up and quickly took her to another room that resembled an operating room.

My husband and I were allowed to sit in this room while lots of people were doing lots of things to our baby girl. It all seemed as if it were a dream – this was not happening. "Lord just let me wake up." It was not a dream.

I prayed over and over sitting there in that room. Gracie was wet with sweat, but yet her temperature was only 94.5 degrees. They had her under a heat lamp to try to warm her up and were bringing in warm blankets that had been heated. They were putting all kinds of needles in her, but she had no response during all of this.

No Cries, No Moves, Nothing

One nurse pulled Gracie's eye lids open and shined a light into them. I later found out, her pupils were fixed. They were not responding to the light. This is often a result of someone who is brain dead! They had no idea what was wrong with Gracie. After some time passed, the doctor wanted to do a spinal tap to see if she had meningitis. When he came in to do this, he asked that we step out of the room.

That test came back negative. They were puzzled as to what was wrong with our little girl. After some time. They prepared to move her to the PICU in critical condition. We were asked to wait in the waiting area. Shortly after getting her into the PICU, a doctor came out and told us that Gracie was having seizures. I then totally broke down, right there in the hallway. My husband went down the hallway and broke down. My mom came out of the waiting area to comfort me, while my dad came out and went to comfort my husband.

How this could be happening, I kept asking over and over again. That Sunday seemed to last an eternity.

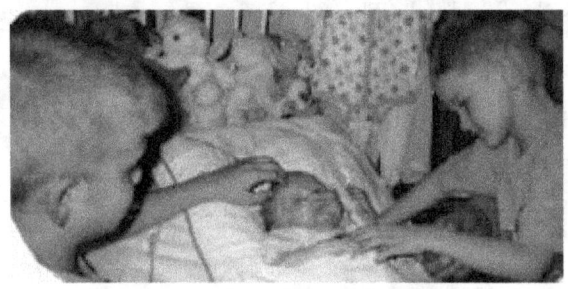

Gracie at 2 weeks old with Brothers Cody and Robert

No Visits

As time passed, they still would not allow us inside the PICU. Oh how I wanted to be by my baby girl's side. The doctor later came out, took my husband and me aside one by one asking if we had any sexually transmitted diseases or anything at all that we could think of that they should know.

We both had answered no, but since they had no idea what was wrong with Gracie, they were trying to rule everything out that they could. Time passed and several family and friends had gathered to be with us. I remember earlier in the day, my sister said let's pray right

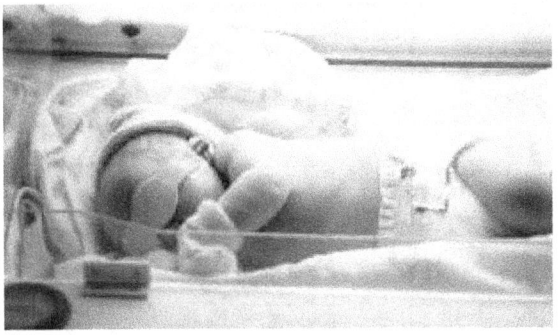

here, right now. So there we were, right there just outside the elevator, praying. Then later, when several from our church had come including our pastor after Sunday evening service was over, they still would allow no one in, so just outside the PICU door we formed a circle, held hands, and prayed. We should pray as if it already is, so we were already thanking God for Gracie's healing.

On Ventilator

By this time, they had Gracie on a ventilator – breathing for her. The doctor on staff that night was a wonderful doctor. I remember clearly one time as he came out to update us, he had tears in his eyes. Although things didn't look so well for our little girl, they continued to do everything possible to save her. We know they were led by God's healing hands. That night was a very long night. Knowing our little girl lie in a coma was so very hard to accept.

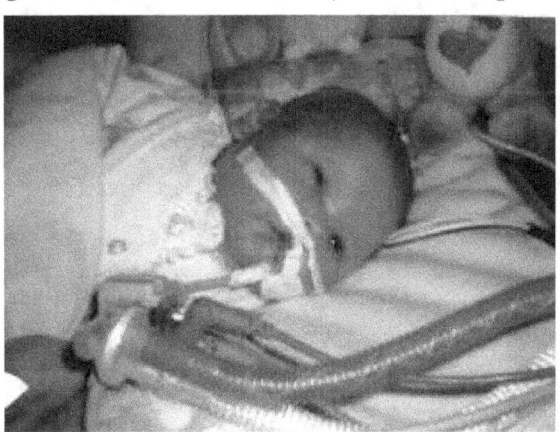

Gracie at 1 week old on life support

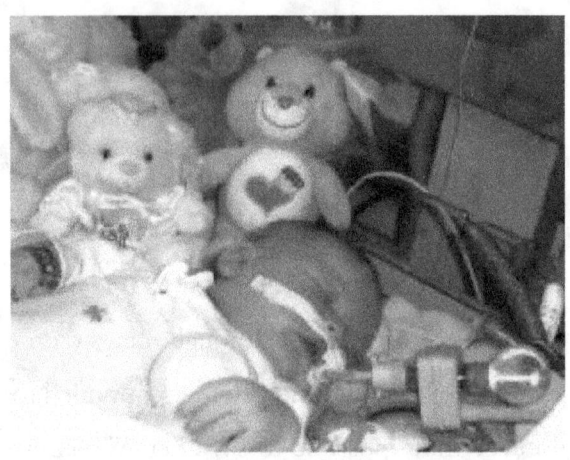

The next day on Monday another doctor came onto duty. He told them to check her ammonia level, they did and found it was very elevated. At its highest point it was over 500. Normal is between 9 and 33. They soon got a diagnosis – Citrullinemia, which is a urea cycle disorder. We were told it's very rare, so rare that a lot of doctors have never even heard of it. They transported her to the University of Tennessee Medical Center where she was the first to receive hemofiltration. This is where a big machine draws blood out of the body, cleans it, then puts the clean blood back into the body.

When they transported her, she was a pale grey color as if she were dead. She was, in fact, near death at that point. She remained at U.T. for a day, then they transported her back to children's. She continued hemofiltration at children's, but on a smaller machine. At one point, Gracie's liver stopped functioning. Knowing we can't survive without our liver, we began focusing our prayers on her liver to begin functioning again. They said they would give her plasma in hopes of boosting her liver. They thought they would have to give her three rounds just to boost it, but after only one round, it was fully functioning again. She had to have blood transfusions as well. We agreed to several studies to be done on Gracie because we had to exercise every possibility to save her. At some point, an EEG was done by a doctor. It did show abnormal. This doctor told us Gracie may never wake up, and if she did she'll never be "normal".

The Hospital is Our Home

My husband and I were always at the hospital. Always at least one of us. My husband never left the hospital for days. He wouldn't even stay at the Ronald McDonald House which was only two blocks away, because he said that was too far away. He was continuously signing consent forms. He was exhausted. I was exhausted but we would have never been anywhere else but by our baby's side. At one point in time, I remember touching her little foot and it moved! My husband and I were excited to see this, but our excitement diminished when we told the nurse, and her response was simply, "I'm sorry, but that was just a reflex." We did not let this discourage us though. My husband had placed pictures of Gracie's brothers and sisters in the little bed she lay in. We would stroke her hair, rub her little body wherever we could. Since she had so many tubes and lines there wasn't a lot of places to touch her. I sang to her. We had a nurse place a radio in the room that played soothing music for her. We continually prayed over her. I remember a time that my mom had placed her hand on Gracie about where her liver was and read scripture over her and we prayed. Our pastor prayed over her. Lots of other people prayed for her, many were limited on coming into the PICU. Gracie's grandfather and Uncle from out of town had drove straight down to be by Gracie's side and to support us. I think they feared they would be attending a funeral upon their arrival.

Restrictions for Gracie

Gracie had been put on a very strict formula recipe that would restrict the protein and also on several medications to help control the ammonia and things that pertain to her disorder.

Gracie on life support

On the third day as I often would do, I stroked the bottom of her foot with my nail, this time it was definitely not a reflex, she moved her foot! Gracie's dad and I were very excited over this. Soon after, by the next day our little girl was beginning to come out of the coma! Praise be to our Lord, our daughter is waking up! Her eyes were so swollen from being on the respirator that although she tried to open them, she could not. We continued to talk to her, sing to her, play music and most importantly, to pray.

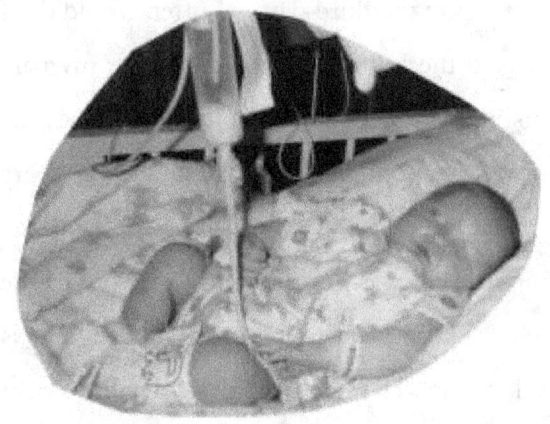

She finally got to where she could open her eyes entirely – then she began to look around, but she didn't do much more than that. She seemed to not move her arms or legs. We were told if a person survives a high ammonia episode such as Gracie's there tends to be brain damage. But we prayed against that. With this disorder Gracie would be required to drink a certain amount of her special formula at a certain time, so therefore a feeding tube was surgically placed into Gracie's belly, so if she didn't take in the certain amount by her bottle it then would have to be tube fed to her. Her formula in a sense was like medicine for her. She also had a port-a-cath surgically placed just above her feeding tube to be used in cases of emergency when Gracie may get a fever, because that can cause the ammonia to get elevated or simply catching a bug could possibly cause it to go up, this way with the port in place, they would immediately have I.V. access to start administering drugs to bring it down. Gracie finally progressed enough to move out of the intensive care and onto a floor. We began to learn how to care for Gracie, with all the medications, how to make her special formula, how to feed her. It was all so very overwhelming. I didn't think I would ever grasp on to all the care that it would involve. There was a lady just prior to Gracie's discharge that came in just to teach us on the feeding tube and all that was involved with that.

Finally after almost a month in the hospital we were allowed to take our little girl home. Home health care had delivered the necessary supplies we would need to care for her. PT, OT, and SP was also set up. Soon after stress did set in, I must admit, with all the demands involved in her care. My husband and I began to snap at one another but soon enough we did settle in and get adjusted to everything so then it just became second nature. We would never complain though because although it was a lot of work, we had our baby with us, and we gave God all the glory.

We Heard it on the Radio

Shortly after all of this happened, my parents heard a song on a gospel radio station. It was called *Thank You Lord for Saving Grace* by the Galloways. My mom said to my dad, if I didn't know better, I'd say that song was written for Gracie. My dad replied, "Maybe it was." So, I knew I had to hear it. I tried to find it at the Christian book store but was told it had to be purchased directly through the Galloways and was given a website. So once we received this CD and heard the song, I knew I had to find out the story behind the song, because this was Gracie's song! I sent an e-mail and the reply to my question was that it was not based on anything that had happened to anyone they knew, just that the song had come to Earl in the group The Galloways and he wanted the group to sing it. So my thought was, as my dad had earlier stated maybe it was written for Gracie. God works in mysterious ways sometimes. This song is truly "Gracie's song" as a matter of fact some of the words in the song are now painted in Gracie's bedroom. This group which is based out of Nashville, Tennessee even came three hours to do a concert at our church for Gracie. We still keep in touch with them, and have told them, they will forever be a part of Gracie's life.

What about a Transplant?

We took Gracie to see a specialist at Vanderbilt Children's Hospital to inquire into a liver transplant for Gracie. This doctor evaluated her and took down information from us, then sent us home with homework of deciding where we would take Gracie because Vanderbilt does not do liver transplants on children. So we went home and studied and decided the best choice would be children's hospital in Philadelphia. We were scheduled to meet with the whole transplant team in January 2005. After meeting with them, they determined Gracie was an excellent candidate for a liver transplant and soon after was placed on their liver transplant list.

The first call for her transplant came only four months after she was placed on the list. Gracie and her dad caught a chartered flight and flew to Pennsylvania. We were all filled with mixed emotions but knew this was the best choice for Gracie to live a longer and a better quality of life. We just hated for her to have to go through it. After many anxious hours it was determined that the donor liver could not be used for Gracie, so she was sent home. The second call came months later, which ended up like the first – Gracie and dad flew to Pennsylvania, hours pass, but this liver could not be used for Gracie and she was sent home. The third call came only a week after the last one, this liver also could not be used for Gracie, but before Gracie left, another liver became available so they wanted her to wait to see about it, more waiting but once again, a fourth liver could not be used for Gracie. We began to wonder how common were the problems that caused the livers to not be able to be used, so we asked the question and were told very uncommon, and with one of the livers where there is an extra vein, that was next to unheard of. So my thought on all that was, that God can see the big picture where we can't and I believe he made obvious reasons for them not to even attempt to place any of them in Gracie. The doctors said they had never called anyone more than 3 times until Gracie.

The Call Came

Several months passed and on February 8, 2006 another call came. This time it was a size match where in the past calls, Gracie would only have gotten half of the liver due to the size. The surgery took 6 to 7 hours, in which Gracie did wonderfully. The surgeons did an excellent job leaving her with a very "neat" scar. Gracie did not need any blood, although we were prepared for her to have to have transfusions. We knew God was in that operating room leading the doctors' hands. We know that God working through the doctors is why everything went extremely well. After the surgery, the doctors told us they had never seen anyone before do as well as quickly as Gracie! Amen, and may all the glory be to God.

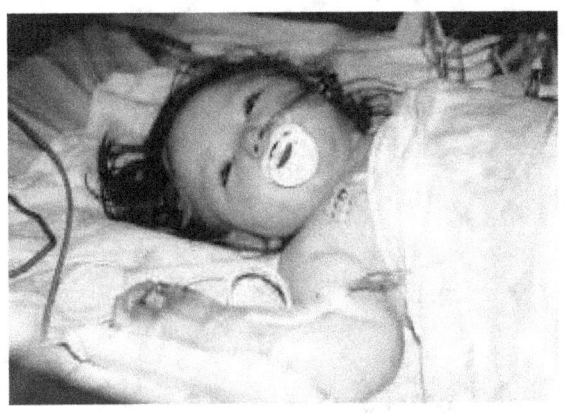

Right after Liver transplant surgery in Philadelphia, Pennsylvania

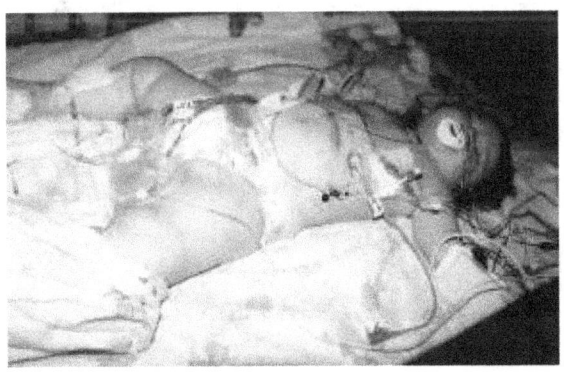

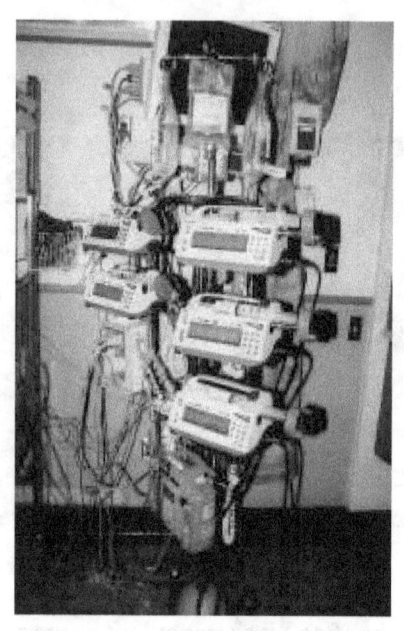

All the I.V. Pumps for Gracie

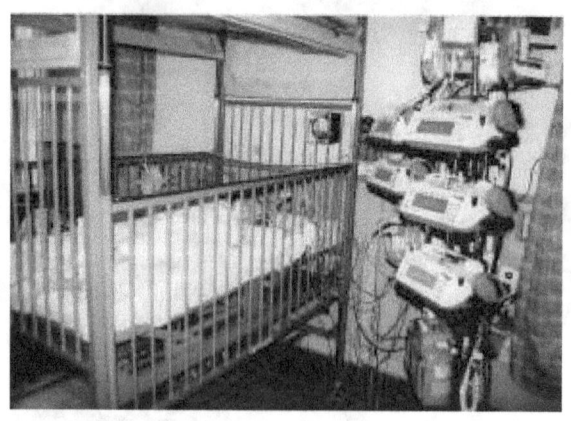

Talk of Discharge

At nine days out, the doctors began to talk of going ahead and discharging Gracie, since she was doing so very well. However, at ten days out Gracie began to reject her new liver. The doctors had told us that fifty percent of recipients do reject. We began to pray even harder for God to work through this for Gracie. They began administering drugs to help her stop rejecting. On day two of these drugs most people have begun to respond, but Gracie did not. Oh how emotional this was, to know our little girl got this wonderful gift of a new liver but now her body was attacking it! Finally on day three, she began responding and her numbers from the labs were although slow they were beginning to come back down. Amen!

After a few more days, Gracie was discharged to the Ronald McDonald House which we stayed for about another week, with doctor visits while there to check labs and all. We spent a total of about a month in Philadelphia. Finally we could bring our little girl home, all healthy as could be. We are so very grateful to the family that gave such a great gift, they gave Gracie the chance to go on and potentially live a very long, healthy life. We still have heard no response from the donor family as we sent them a thank you card and letter shortly after the transplant, our plan is to continue to send them a card of our appreciation and let them know how their gift has helped her. Maybe someday they will respond to us, but even if they never do they will always be in our thoughts, hearts and prayers.

Once we got home with Gracie I was a bit nervous, I thought if she were to go into rejection again, how will we know, I decided to pray on it, put it in God's hands, and leave it there. Sometimes we often want to pray on something but instead of leaving it with God, we pick it right back up and take it with us. I admit I often fail at this, but I decided to let God take over and if Gracie were to be in trouble, God would let us know.

Finally Home

It felt so good to finally be back home, in our own beds, to get back to our "normal" way of life, but only four days later Gracie was running a fever, which can be a sign of rejection, so I called the doctors in Philadelphia who said to get her to our local children's emergency room, they called them to give them the heads up of our coming and what to do. Once there, and with lots of communicating between the doctors there and the doctors in Philadelphia they wanted antibiotics started right away among other things.

Once we were put in a room Gracie immediately began to cry as if to say, no not again. She was so over doctors and hospitals. When labs began to come back they revealed she in fact was not in rejection, so that was a huge relief, but she had something going on but they couldn't pin point it. Her blood level began to drop, and needed a transfusion, which went smoothly, Gracie accepted the blood with no complications. They tested her port-a-cath thinking it may have become infected but it was negative. They ran other tests and asked us lots of questions, but kept coming up empty handed. So they decided to go ahead and remove her port just in case it was the culprit, although the labs said it was not. Once they removed it in surgery, her fever went away so they felt that could have been the problem. Also prior to transplant Gracie tested negative for CMV (cytomegalovirus), but the liver she received tested positive. They now discovered she tested positive for CMV. I don't understand CMV completely, except that about 80 percent of us by age 40 do test positive for it so most people don't even know it. Gracie has had another brief hospital stay and lots of doctor visits, labs, tests, etc. but all in all she is doing wonderful. She continues to get therapy and although she's delayed we are confident she will do what she's supposed to but even if she doesn't she will be loved no less. She has brought so much inspiration to so many. When we want to complain about a little ache or a little shot, we think of Gracie and all that she's been through and how very tough she is. We don't know what the future holds for any of us, but we do know that we must take one day at a time and cherish what we have, because we were not promised tomorrow. And although God didn't promise us days without storms he did promise us he'd be with us through the storms.

Update

The donor family has responded several times and even sent a picture of the little boy who was only 3yrs old and died from a house fire, and his mother had wrapped him in a blanket to help protect him. She passed out from smoke inhalation and was in a coma for two weeks. His grandmother gave consent to donate his organs.

We keep the framed picture of him in our livingroom. Although we celebrate every February 8th as the day Gracie received the gift of life. We remember that for the donor family it is a memorial day.

Gracie will soon be 10years old and to this day remains nonverbal. However, she communicates in other ways. We have communication devices--placed throughout our home-- that she pushes and a recording plays. For example, I want to go outside or please change my television channel, she often takes our hands and leads us to what she wants. Her nightly communication device when pressed says, "Good night, I love you." She presses this for each one of us before going to bed.

Gracie continues to be tube fed. Currently her doctor at Vanderbilt Children's Hospital is trying to get her into a very intense, inpatient 8 week long feeding therapy program in Maryland. Gracie also continues to be incontinent of both bladder and bowel.

Our prayer is that Gracie will someday be able to eat, drink and get rid of her feeding tube, be continent and maybe even find her voice. We realize our Gracie will never grow up and move away, so that means we'll never be empty nesters. I'm okay with that because God gave us this child and she's ours.

Early on I questioned why me but now I say why not me. For God is good all the time, all the time God is good!

Amen!

The Schommer Family

Gracie and her mother, Julie, ready for church

Update – September 2018

Gracie is now 14 years old. She has made a lot of improvements. She has found her "voice," what I mean by that is, she still does not have the ability to speak, however she "speaks" to us in other ways, in some ways a stranger would not understand what she's trying to communicate but to us we know. For example, if the particular DVD she wants is not in the case she's looking through she will close it then take our hand and motion in the direction of her other DVD case (she has two).

She also now has a communication device known as proxtalker, when different pictures are placed on a certain spot then pressed it speaks what the picture is. For example, "I love you", "yes"," no", "all done", "goodnight". She also has a program called prologue on her iPad, that works somewhat like her proxtalker only it's a program, she often swipes to go to the pictures that say, "I want to", "watch the parade". Gracie loves watching the Macy day parade and other similar parades.

Next month (Oct) will mark 1 year that Lily came into Gracie's life. Lily is Gracie's service dog. Lily will soon be 3 years old. She's a golden retriever, she's just like any other dog, that is until her vest is on, because you see when her vest is on that means she's working she is a completely different dog. She has a job to do when her vest is on and that's to serve Gracie. Her job is to give Gracie freedom all while keeping Gracie safe. You see Gracie has no fears and does not know safety. When Lily is working for Gracie there is a tether that goes from Gracie to Lily, the service dog, so she can't wonder off into danger. It allows Gracie freedom, giving her a sense of independence, all while remaining safe.

Gracie is currently in middle school as a special ed 7th grader. We were concerned about the transition to the middle school from the elementary school, but we prayed about it and praise the Lord the transition was smooth, and Gracie has great teachers and a wonderful attendant.

She has participated in special Olympics now several times, twice for bowling and twice for track and field (walking) once throwing a softball, and this year later this month she will participate in aquatic special Olympics.

Gracie continues to amaze us and continues to progress, and we continue to give God all the glory!

Update - September 2022

Gracie is now 18 years old! She's an adult! Just to think the doctors didn't think she'd survive as an infant and now she's an adult!

She still continues to progress and will still find ways to amaze us. We, of course, give God all the glory.

Grace has now transitioned to the high school, and that is going well. We give most of the credit to her amazing attendant, Tracy. Tracy is not only he attendant, she teaches her and guides her daily. We thank God for her often – for without her in Gracie's life, I don't think she'd be where she is today.

Gracie no longer uses her proxtalker communication device, except just before bedtime to tell me goodnight and she loves me. She instead uses her iPad with the prologue app to communicate and she uses it very well now. When you ask her a yes or no question, she often presses her answer 3 times in a row, so we will hear, "No, no, no" or "Yes, yes, yes."

Grace now has 3 nieces, Aria, Hazel and Stella which she doesn't like to share with but reluctantly agrees to.

She continues to amaze us, and we continue to thank God fo his hand on her life.

If you would like to know any additional information on Gracie's story, feel free to email me at schommermom@aol.com and put "Gracie" in the subject line.

About the Author

The author was born Julie Sims in January of 1971, and she was raised in Knoxville, Tennessee by two wonderful, loving parents.

She is married to a loving, Christian man, Paul, and they have six children in which one, Justin, is in Heaven, then they have Lauren, Brittany, Cody, Robert and their baby girl, Gracie. Their two oldest girls live on their own. The Schommer's live in Loudon, Tennessee.

Julie was blessed to be a stay at home mother for many years, but now she works in the medical field and has for some time. She has learned more from raising Gracie than she thinks she ever did in school.

Schommermom@aol.com

**Gracie and Bruce Pearl.
Gracie as Tennessee Donor Poster Child**

www.ingramcontent.com/pod-product-compliance
Lightning Source LLC
Chambersburg PA
CBHW052207110526
44591CB00012B/2121